Stunt Flyers

Written by Lucy Armour

Contents

Stunt Flyers

Stunt flyers are pilots who do amazing moves, or stunts, with their planes. Some pilots perform the stunts on their own. Others perform them together in groups of planes. This is called formation flying.

Pilots began stunt flying in World War I. They had to be very skilled at flying their planes. They learned stunts to help them avoid being attacked. After the war, the pilots performed the stunts they had learned at air shows. They would show off their stunts to crowds of people.

Today, people still enjoy watching air shows all over the world.

How Pilots Perform the Stunts

Stunt flyers move their planes in three different ways to do the stunts. These three moves are called roll, pitch and yaw.

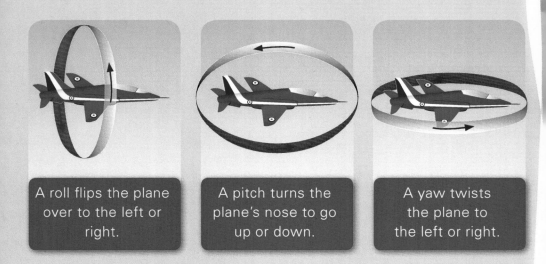

A roll flips the plane over to the left or right.

A pitch turns the plane's nose to go up or down.

A yaw twists the plane to the left or right.

Roll

To make a plane roll, the pilot uses the wing flaps. The pilot has a control stick, called a yoke, to move the wing flaps.

The "barrel roll" is a type of roll stunt. The pilot rolls the plane over and over in a corkscrew pattern as the plane speeds forwards.

down

up

down

If the pilot turns the yoke to the left, the left wing flap goes up and the right wing flap goes down. This rolls the plane to the left.

If the pilot turns the yoke to the right, the right wing flap goes up, the left wing flap goes down and the plane rolls to the right.

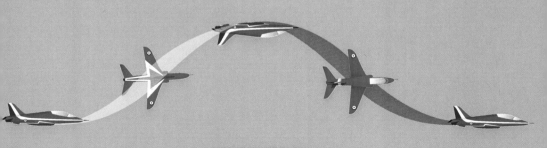

barrel roll

Pitch

To make a plane pitch, the pilot uses the flaps on the tail of the plane. The tail flaps can move up and down. The yoke controls the tail flaps.

The "loop" is a type of pitch stunt. The pilot pitches the plane up or down and flies it in a circle.

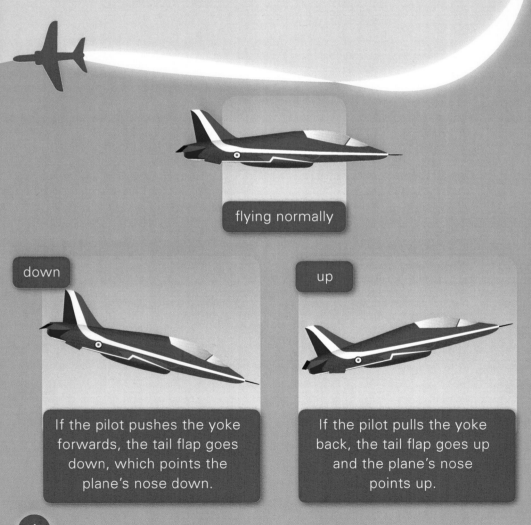

flying normally

down

up

If the pilot pushes the yoke forwards, the tail flap goes down, which points the plane's nose down.

If the pilot pulls the yoke back, the tail flap goes up and the plane's nose points up.

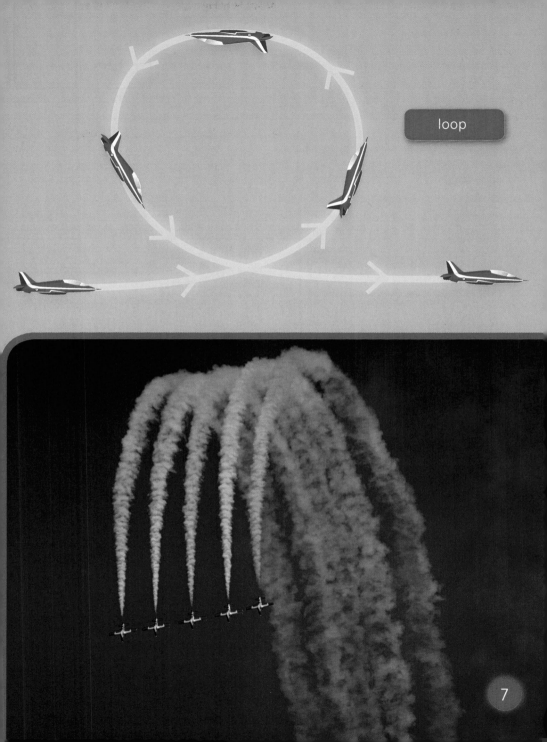

loop

Yaw

To make a plane yaw, the pilot uses the rudder on the tail of the plane. The pilot uses two foot pedals to move the rudder.

The "stall turn" is a stunt that uses yaw. The pilot flies the plane straight up until it slows. Then the pilot yaws the plane to the left or right until the nose faces the ground. The plane speeds down again.

right

If the pilot presses the right pedal, the rudder swings to the right and the plane yaws to the right.

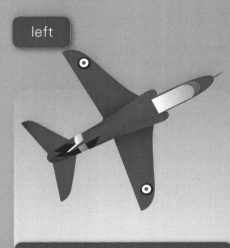

left

If the pilot presses the left foot pedal, the rudder swings to the left and the plane yaws to the left.

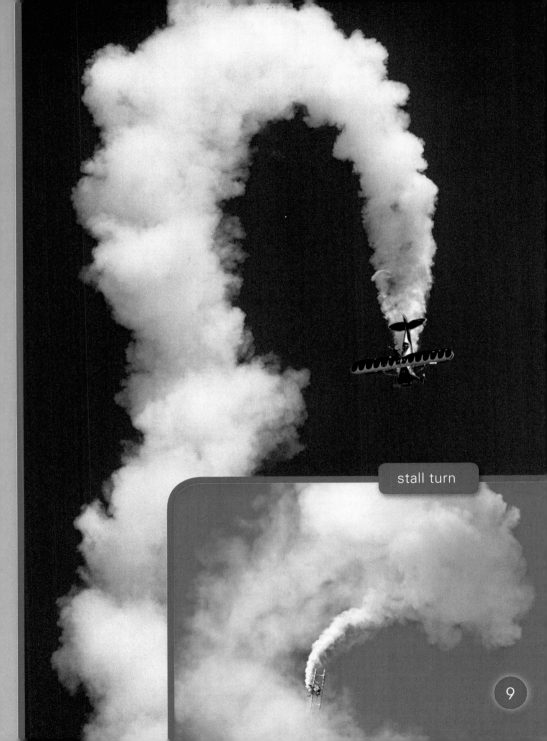

stall turn

9

Flying Together

When stunt pilots fly their planes together, it is called formation flying. They can do amazing stunts in a group. They often let smoke out of the backs of their planes to make patterns in the sky.

The Red Arrows is a famous group of stunt flyers. There are nine planes in the Red Arrows. These are some of their formations.

This formation is called the "diamond nine". The planes form the shape of a diamond. It is the Red Arrows' most famous move.

This formation is called the "wineglass". Planes 2, 3, 4 and 5 move up and planes 8 and 9 move back to form the shape of a wineglass.

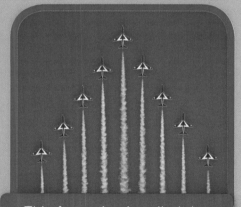

This formation is called the "big nine". Planes 4, 5, 8 and 9 move back and out. Planes 6 and 7 move up and out to form the shape of an arrow.

This formation is called the "feathered arrow.. Planes 8 and 9 move back to form the shape of a feathered arrow.

The Red Arrows change formation all the time during an air show. This is one of their famous moves. It is called a "wineglass roll". The planes form a wineglass. Then they do a barrel roll. As they come out of the barrel roll, they form a feathered arrow.

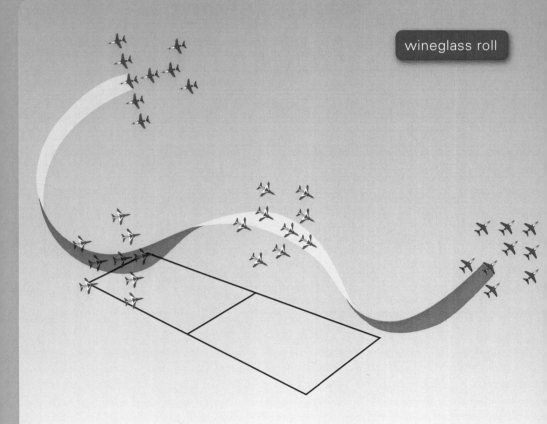

wineglass roll

This move is called a "feathered arrow loop". The planes start in a feathered arrow. Then they do a loop. As they come out of the loop, they form a nine arrow.

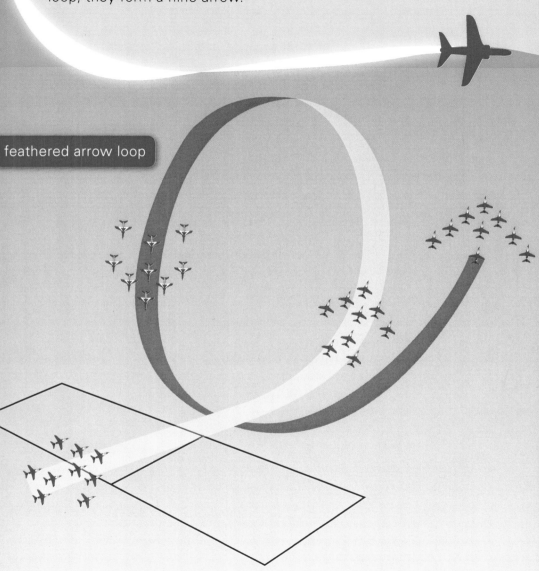

feathered arrow loop

The Dangers of Stunt Flying

Stunt flying can be very dangerous. The planes often fly very close to the ground and other planes, so one wrong move can cause a crash. Stunts flyers have been badly hurt or killed in the past.

Many modern stunt planes have an escape system. If the pilot knows the plane will crash, they can fire the ejection seat. First, the glass over the cockpit shatters away from the pilot. Then a rocket fires the pilot's seat into the air, away from the plane. A parachute attached to the seat opens and the pilot floats safely to the ground.

pilot ejects

How the ejection seat works

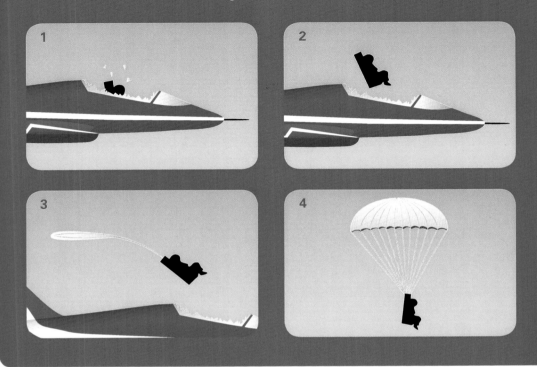

1

2

3

4

plane about to crash

plane explodes

Glossary

cockpit: the area in a plane where the pilots sit

ejection seat: a pilot's seat that can be fired out of a plane

feathered arrow: an arrow with a feather at its tail

yoke: a control stick used to steer a plane

Index

Stunt Flyers is an **Explanation**.

An explanation explains **how** and **why** things happen.

An explanation has a topic:

Stunt Flyers

An explanation has headings:

How Pilots Perform Stunts

Flying Together

The Dangers of Stunt Flying

Some information is put under headings.

The Dangers of Stunt Flying

- planes fly very close together
- planes fly close to the ground
- pilots can be hurt or killed.

Information can be shown in other ways.
This explanation has …

Labels   Captions   Photographs   Illustrations

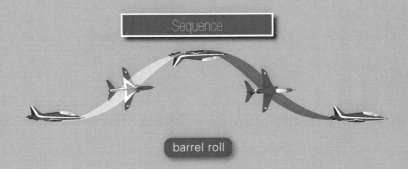

Sequence

barrel roll

Guide Notes

Title: Stunt Flyers

Stage: Fluency

Text Form: Informational Explanation

Approach: Guided Reading

Processes: Thinking Critically, Exploring Language, Processing Information

Written and Visual Focus: Contents Page, Labels, Captions, Index, Glossary, Illustrations, Sequence Diagrams

THINKING CRITICALLY
(sample questions)

Before Reading – Establishing Prior Knowledge
- What do you know about stunt flyers?

Visualising the Text Content
- What might you expect to see in this book?
- What form of writing do you think will be used by the author?

Look at the contents page and index. Encourage the students to think about the information and make predictions about the text content.

After Reading – Interpreting the Text
- Do you think formation flying is difficult? Why do you think that?
- Why do you think it is important for stunt flyers to be very fit and strong?
- What is the most important thing about being a stunt flyer? Why do you think that?
- Why do you think people like going to air shows to watch stunt flyers?
- Do you think being a stunt flyer is an exciting job? Why do you think that?
- What do you know about stunt flyers that you didn't know before?
- What things in the book helped you to understand the information?
- What questions do you have after reading the text?

EXPLORING LANGUAGE

Terminology
Photograph credits, index, contents page, imprint information, ISBN number